Inside a King's Mind

By Benjamin Jones Jr.

This book is dedicated to my beloved mother, Cynthia Jones, for raising me to be a strong man and understanding my purpose in life.

Mrs. Cynthia Jones

December 8, 1956 – December 4, 2006

ACKNOWLEDGMENTS

I would first like to thank my heavenly father for making it possible for me to share my words of inspiration to everyone who reads this book, my Queen and backbone for always believing and helping me discover my purpose in life, and my beautiful daughter, Journee, whom I love always and embrace with my unconditional love that no one can break. I would also like to thank my tutor, mentor, and friend, Ms. Riggins, who always taught me to reach my highest potential and helping me to get this far. I'd like to thank my friend Bro. Marcus, Barry, Ashton, James, Jeff, Kareem, Patrick, Nicole, and all my siblings for having my back. I would like to thank everyone for supporting this book, and I hope these poems give you clarity and guide you to your purpose in life.

CONTENTS

CHAPTER 1

Love and Relationships

Love at First Sight

Since the first time we met,

It was love at first sight.

I remember like it was yesterday, on that warm summer night.

I knew you were the one, so I made my first move,

Hesitant at first, but my conscience told me just be you.

Before I opened my mouth, you reached and told me your name,

As nervous I was, likewise I did the same,

From that moment on, we established a foundation,

A connection so strong that only God can break it.

We honored an oath to sacrifice our freedom for each other's heart

This will always allow me to shine my light in your dark.

Only our heavenly father knows where we go from here,

No matter what, my unconditional love will never disappear.

Who is this Woman?

Who is this woman I'm lying next to?

I can't remember how we met,

But only the memories of me making love to you.

The mysterious thoughts take control of my mind,

Our body language speaks words only we can define.

I embrace our presence in each other's company.

I'm feeling like a new man

With so much pressure that's been relieved.

What we did in our world will never be exposed,

But only time will reveal WHO KNOWS?

Man

A man is a provider

Who never makes excuses.

He always expresses his emotions

With the frustration of losing,

In a world with a lack of opportunities.

But he has the power

To control what's not included.

He maintains his hope and reps his team.

But most of all,

He never stops believing.

CHAPTER 2

Spirituality

Sovereignty

The light covers the dark,

Your love flows through my heart.

The truth appears on my face

With the many blessings I receive each day.

Rain may pour, but the moon glows

With the guidance in your faith,

I continue to move on.

CHAPTER 3

Enlightenment and Empowerment

Follow Me

If only I can return to a historical moment in the past,

Explaining to my fellow brothers and sisters

The light that shines with guidance from the moonlight.

This shall navigate you directly to freedom

Without being afraid of losing the fight;

Focus on your heart which pumps courage into your soul.

I know your greatest potential,

And nothing can destroy what our king has planned,

Despite what the masses consider

Only God knows the truth which lives in you.

Transition

For a long time,

I understood the importance of moving on,

With the intentions of leaving everything behind,

For not benefiting my future.

Searching for an identity in a world not designed for me,

But only conquering the obstacles in place

And striving for the truth.

My childhood neighborhood

Wouldn't be considered a magical community.

It was only a lost city with dreams

Of becoming a heaven of peace.

So I say to you,

Your education and persistence

Will land you where you need to be,

But only the strong will continue to be set free.

Graduation Day

The time has come for what I did,

Many hours studying was worth every minute invested.

$50,000 in debt was the best purchase I ever made.

Red Bull and Pandora gave me strength to keep moving,

Full of energy to keep pursuing.

I walked on stage, and my name was announced loud.

Looking at my Queen, as she glanced and smiled.

Thank you for the time.

I express my gratitude.

Strive for greatness, and you shall achieve too.

Philosophy of a King

The truth of my vision will only release tension,

With the upsetting corruption in the world,

I will navigate you to your natural pearl.

The leadership of someone

Who believes in greatness will help structure your mind

With the understanding of being patient.

Levitate your soul pumping your heart of gold.

No need to shout,

For in time everyone will know

Exactly what it's all about.

Keep Moving

Life is impenetrable,

Trying to live in a delusional world.

Deciding on what path to take and the next move to make.

Visions are blurry,

Not even with prescription frames can see through the pain.

Only God's will can lead you to the promised land.

Self –confident and eager to endure imaginable pleasure,

But this illusion has me under pressure.

If the weights pull you down,

Push hard as you crawl on the ground.

It's true:

What doesn't kill you,

Only makes you only stronger.

It's now the time to let loose and run,

For I can't hold on no longer.

Over-Achiever

Considering my intentions on my next move

Understanding my purpose in life

And why I continue make boss moves.

Narrow-minded folks will never get my drift,

Quick to point's fingers,

But won't clap their hands for my accomplishments.

Advancing my knowledge and giving credit

To James Baldwin leaving America.

Stepping out on faith and hoping

One day your story

Will lead our generation in a fair equality nation.

Epistemology Mind

Expand my knowledge.

Feeding me truth will help grow my mind.

Not eliminating false junk will only make me sick over time.

My circumstance will not define me,

But each second, I'm playing Russian roulette,

Having negative pressure build in my chest.

It's my purpose to lead my flock

Where the weather is unconditional,

But love will always be my prediction of the day.

Epistemology King

The untold truth

From what needs to be known,

Figuring how to survive

In an unexceptional world

Will retrieve your falsely title rocks into pearls.

Invest in yourself,

For what will soon change the world.

Dealing with the actions of people.

What's your Purpose?

This is the question I ask myself every day?

Why am I here?

Who cares about me? Am I free?

These age-old questions drive me to believe

That I'm here to contribute to the world as precious as a pearl.

I really don't know,

So I guess the only option is to travel wherever the wind blows.

Every day is routine;

The pattern of getting ready for work

And providing for my family.

It really has to be more to life than doing

What you must do, opposite of what you want to do.

OK?

Whets next what step,

I guess something must be left.

I will find out in time,

But for now,

I'm going too aim directly at the sky.

Benjamin Expectations

I promised myself I would never give-up on myself,

This has already been a rocky journey,

Unfolding the simplest assignments.

Vultures respond you are too old,

You have a daughter,

You're incompetent, and you're not fit for that.

Looking past of all what they consider

My downfall is only motivating me to reach higher elevation,

With all my potential to accomplish what God has planned for me.

The truth, what I believe,

Will set me free from my upbringing.

Circumstances and rough

Encounters in the past have pushed me to strive and survive.

CHAPTER 4

Childhood Memories

Where I'm From

Living in a place, the opposite of comfort,

The feeling of loneliness is what it has to offer.

Deep inside, you feel no one cares,

Just the lost minds of people

Don't know why they are there.

No motivational, no role models,

Only false fantasies of drug dealers

And top models with surgical 50,000 dollar bodies.

I was once told to wake up and stop feeling hopeless

Because with that attitude no doors will open.

I slowly realized that it was a test

For you to learn from your flaws and upbringing,

Which will gradually move you in a positive direction.

I'm not trying to sell you a false hope.

I just want you to know it's time to move on,

NOW LET'S GO . . .

CHAPTER 5

Family Matters

Fatherhood

The moments we share,

I never would have cared,

About your imperfection,

For our flaws are life-learned lessons.

Even if your mother and I part ways

Forever I stay.

Giving up with an invalid excuse will never be used,

For I am the energy that flows through you.

Daddy loves you,

From the earth to the moon,

For you I will always be true.

CHAPTER 6

Mixed Emotions

Accept Me for Who I Am

The truth is

I'm just playing a game,

Fabricating this person you see.

I really don't care anymore who don't like me.

Everyone points fingers to dim my light.

Many times, I want to be forgotten without a fight.

Some consider me bitter.

I'm not appealing for my medical condition.

Self-esteem low and one will never know.

No longer will I share thoughts of inspiring tales,

Truth is,

No one cares.

Borrowed Time

Investing in my life,

But missing out with my loved ones.

It's hard to balance all, but I cannot fall.

There are moments I feel overwhelmed by wanting to stop it all,

But what doesn't kill you, only makes you stronger

If you hold on just a little longer.

My only vision is to dedicate and commit to finish my degree,

But I'm the only one who believes in me.

I'm not throwing a pity party or wanting your sympathy.

It's just exhausting to try and fight this battle

With no support from so-called loved ones to support me.

I will continue to play this game

Until I achieve only what I believe.

Borrowed time is what is offered to me,

But it's what keeps me at peace.

Champions Never Lose

You're the blood flowing my veins,

When we're exposed to a wound,

We heal each other's pain.

I'm the air that you breathe in your lungs,

To filter the toxins for whatever harm or pollution comes.

I'm at the moment in life when you accomplish your goals.

I'm the question to your answer that was reveal and unfold.

I'm your guidance on your trail when you are lost.

I'm the energy when you feel exhausted

And the boost of faith, knowing you will make it.

I'm your soul when you feel lifeless and it's time to go.

I will forever be with you.

I just wanted you to know.

ABOUT THE AUTHOR

Benjamin Jones is a Savannah, Georgia native and enjoys spending time with his wife, Chiquita, and daughter, Journee. He was inspired to write poetry as a teenager experiencing childhood struggles. Benjamin is also an avid golfer and a recent graduate of Embry Riddle University.

Chiquita and Journee Jones

"The most important things in the world are family and love."

-John Wooden